THE GREAT INVENTIONS

CONTENTS

MOONLIGHT PUBLISHING

Just think how many inventions and discoveries there have been since the days of the first cavemen! This book would not exist if reading and writing had not been invented. Before you picked it up, hundreds of people had worked on this book. Some of the techniques they used were invented several centuries ago, some are very modern.

Thousands of years have passed since people first learned to mill flour and make use of the strength of animals.

First, the paper was made. Then the text was written, by hand or with the help of a word processor. The pictures were drawn and coloured. Photographic colour plates were made from them. Once they had been printed and bound, the books were loaded into lorries and delivered to the publisher who sold them to the bookshops. If you bought this copy, you probably used banknotes and coins. Money is another of the great inventions.

People began to build primitive houses for shelter.

Just imagine for a moment what life must have been like ten thousand years ago!

There was no money, no writing, no electric light, no wheels or engines to take you from one place to another... All these inventions which we take for granted now, have transformed the way we look at the world. Sitting in our comfortable houses, we do not worry about heat or cold. Pain and distances are no longer the problems they once were, for now we have central heating, medicines, the telephone and aeroplanes.

The very first discoveries and inventions

Ten thousand years ago, our ancestors had already invented the bow and arrow and the spear to hunt animals for food and clothing. They were beginning to domesticate* the ox and the horse, and they had probably built simple rafts to cross rivers. But, most important of all, they had discovered fire. Discovered, and not invented, for fire exists in Nature; think of the forest fires that are caused by lightning.

Even today, South American Indians are skilful hunters and fishermen using a bow and arrow.

Many civilisations thought that fire was sacred, a gift from the gods.

First people learned to keep a fire going, then how to start one by rubbing stones or pieces of dry wood together to make a spark. They began using fire to cook bread, to forge* tools and weapons, or to bake pottery for storing grain or oil. Soon people were swapping the extra corn they did not need for goods they could not supply themselves: trade had been born.

Barter was the first form of trade.

What does barter mean?
If you swap some marbles for some stickers, or a rubber for some sweets, then you're bartering with your friends! It means exchanging things of similar value.

Barter was the first form of trade.
In the illustration below on the right, you can see an Egyptian farmer exchanging a goose, which he has raised on the farm, for a clay pot in a market. In Ancient Egypt, money did not exist.

Bartering has gone on since very early times.

What are coins, bank notes, cheques and credit cards used for? To buy things, of course. They are all forms of money. You can exchange money for things you cannot produce yourself: books and toys, food or clothes...electricity, travel by bus or by train. **Nowadays, money is used for all kinds of business and trade.** You may still hear people talking about silver and coppers, although coins are no longer made from pure precious metals. Now you can pay not only with coins but with cheques, postal orders and plastic cards, too. But let's take a look at how money came to be invented...

Two cockerels are handed...

from person to person as each man...

exchanges them for something he wants.

Some of the goods that were used as money were rather bulky, like these slabs of copper used by the Phoenicians*.

All over Africa, cowrie shells were used as money for a long time. They were light and easy to count.

The trouble with bartering is that no item has a definite value. What could the Egyptian farmer do if the potter did not want his goose, or if he demanded something else as well? And with the barter system it was impossible to ever make any saving! There had to be another way...

How money began

Throughout history, different societies have chosen different things to use as money. People have used dried fish, bars of salt, cooking pots, cattle... Whatever was chosen had a fixed value. A sword might be worth two head of oxen, a jar of wine only one. But soon it became clear that using pieces of precious metal, which could be cut up and weighed, was really much more practical.

In Ancient Rome, the value of goods was measured in cattle.

What were the coins made from?

Most often from gold, silver and copper. All three of these metals can be found in the ground in a pure state, not hidden within another mineral. They are known as native metals. They do not wear down easily, and are rare; even a tiny piece of gold is worth a great deal.

It was not long before gold became the symbol of wealth.

It glitters as it catches the light, and it is easy to work into different shapes and patterns. The quest for gold led men like Christopher Columbus to unknown, distant lands. In Peru, in South America, the Spanish conquistadores looted the gold and silver of the Inca Indians, and exploited their mineral mines.

Aztec Indians in South America used cocoa beans as money. One rabbit might be worth ten beans.

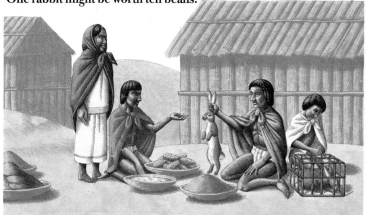

Gold and silver nuggets were made into coins.

A gold nugget and one of Croesus' gold coins

As rich as Croesus!

Croesus was the king of Lydia, now part of Turkey. He was famous for his riches, and it was he who invented coins. Nuggets* of gold and silver were hammered into shape, then stamped with a mark to show what they were worth. There was no longer any need to weigh them. Trade with other countries became much simpler.

Cretan coin   Carthaginian coin   Athenian coin

The Ancient Persians, Greeks and Romans also minted their own coins.

The designs they used tell us about their history. Coins from Ancient Crete showed the famous maze at Knossos. The people of Athens stamped their coins with an owl, which was sacred to their goddess Athena.

The river Pactolus flows through Lydia. Here, people are collecting nuggets of electrum, a mixture of gold and silver.

In Ancient Greece, the silver mines were worked by slaves.

Coins made by craftsmen were copied by crooks!

How did people make coins in the old days?

Below you can see a workshop in the Middle Ages. The coins are first cut from sheets of metal, then struck between two engraved tools which press the design onto them. In those days, a lot of people made coins, but their quality varied. Money-changers had the job of checking the coins. They would tap them to see if they rang true, and weigh them on scales. Good coins were sound and full weight.

There were certain drawbacks to having coins made of real gold and silver.

Counterfeiters would copy the coins and make imitation ones out of metal of no value. If they were caught, these people could be put to death!
Clippers would scrape and file the coins to obtain slivers of the precious metal, which they would then sell.

Heavy, screw-down coin-presses like this one were first used in the 12th century. Nowadays, coins are pressed on a machine powered by electricity.

Since the 17th century, coins have had a clear-cut edge, sometimes grooved, to stop people filing them down. This modern Italian coin is made from two different metals.

Coins today have a lower value than they had in the past.

We use cheques and credit cards to pay large sums of money. Coins are useful for smaller purchases. They are no longer made from precious metals, but from alloys of copper, nickel, brass, palladium. Look at a coin: you will see its value, lettering showing the currency of the country, and the date when it was put into circulation. On British coins, one side shows the Queen's head, the other side a symbol of Britain. Check your money box! Some of the coins may be quite old!

As goods were traded around the world, money spread too.

In the old days, money-changers did many of the jobs of a modern bank.

They kept their customers' money in a safe place, or invested it so that it increased.

1. A customer pays for goods with money.
2. The shopkeeper deposits the money and receives a bill of exchange.
3. The bill could be used to pay another merchant.
4. The bill can be exchanged for coins again.

The word bank comes from banco, the Italian word for the money-changer's bench.

Robbers of course were always after the gold and silver coins. They would waylay travellers to steal their money. It soon became much safer for a merchant to leave his money in the care of a banker. In return, the banker would hand over a signed piece of paper: a bill of exchange. The merchant could use this bill to pay for other goods. Whoever had the bill of exchange could come to the banker in his turn, and exchange it for the original sum of money.

Bank notes, cheques, credit cards: all have stemmed from the original idea of a bill of exchange. As well as bankers, there were money-lenders who charged interest* rates which were often impossibly high. They were called usurers, and they were very unpopular.

The Pont-au-Change in Paris

In 1141, the French King Louis VII ordered that all the gold and silversmiths and money-changers should set up their counters along a bridge over the River Seine. It is called the Pont-au-Change, (Exchange Bridge). The money-changers were in charge of the purity of the coins.

Bank notes: pieces of paper representing the value of gold

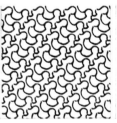

In each country, the artist creates the design, the engraver works it on a metal plate. The note is printed recto verso (front and back).

The background design of each bank note is individually created by computer.   A water-mark

At first, bank notes represented a sum of gold or silver which had been handed into the bank for safekeeping.

The amount of precious coins in the bank exactly equalled the bank notes being used in business. Whoever had a bank note could be sure of being able to exchange it at the bank for pieces of gold. Sometimes bankers would cheat and print more bank notes than they had gold! When the fraud was discovered, they would go bankrupt: they were ruined.

Nowadays, only one bank, the Central Bank in each country, can issue bank notes. It supervises the banking system. In balance to the notes in circulation, the Central Bank holds gold, bank notes from other countries, known as foreign currency, and other valuable items.

Bank notes were soon widely used. There was no time limit to them, and all shops and businesses accepted them.

The making of a bank note is a delicate operation!

The note has to be very difficult to copy. It is made from special paper. If you hold it up to the light, you will see the design of the water-mark through it. Many colours of ink are used, and sometimes even invisible ink. The printing process is kept secret!

When the bank notes become too dirty, torn, or damaged, they are exchanged for new ones by the banks, and then destroyed.

It was the Chinese who began using paper money in the 9th century. The first bank notes carried the seal of the Emperor.

Many people in France were ruined when the financier, John Law, went bankrupt in the 18th century. There were riots on the streets.

Money all over the world

The smallest bank note in the world came from Morocco. It was the size of a postage stamp.

Every country has its own particular money: its currency.

You can exchange one national currency for another. To make this possible, banks have to set up the exchange rate between the currencies of different countries. It varies every day depending how strong the economy* of the country is.

These days, most people put their money in a bank.

Why? Because it is safe, and the bank can offer a range of other services. When you deposit money in a bank, you are given a cheque book, which is a convenient way to pay. Banks can also lend you money.

Security firms transport large sums of money in armoured vehicles.

You may have seen your parents writing a cheque. They fill in the date, the amount they want to pay, and the name of the person to whom they are paying the cheque, and then they sign it, to prove they wish to make the payment. When the cheque is handed over to the bank by the payee, the bank takes that amount of money from your parents' bank account, and pays it to the person whose name is on the cheque.

The currency of the United States is the dollar.

The currency of Japan is the yen.

The currency of Belgium is the Belgian franc.

The currency of Germany is the Deutschmark.

The currency of Italy is the lira.

The currency of France is the French franc.

The currency of Spain is the peseta.

The currency of Holland is the florin.

The currency of Great Britain is the pound.

Credit cards: a convenient way to pay for expensive items

Often banks have a strongroom where their clients can store money, jewels or other valuables.

A bank allows you to pay by credit.

If your parents do not have enough money to buy a house or a car, the bank may lend them some: this is called credit. In exchange for this service, your parents will have to pay back the bank a sum slightly larger than the sum they borrowed. The difference between the two sums is called interest.

What are credit cards?

These plastic cards can be used like cheques. On the back of each card, you will see a magnetic band. This contains the card's memory, which allows it to identify the account from which the money is to be taken. Some countries are beginning to use smart cards, which have a built-in computer. They will record every purchase we make – even a newspaper! You can also use a plastic card to draw money from a cash machine in the wall of a bank, but for security reasons, these machines can only dispense a certain amount of cash.

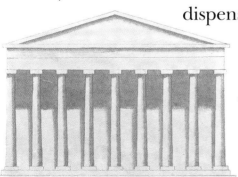

The *Bourse*, the French Stock Exchange*, was designed to look like a Greek temple. Bourse means purse in French.

The secret code in the card's memory is hidden in the magnetic band.

You can use your credit card to draw money from automatic cash machines, but first you have to type in the special secret number which corresponds to your own card.

Most people work to earn a living. In return for our work, we are paid money.

We deposit the money with a bank. The bank opens an account for us, and gives us a cheque book and cheque card.

We can pay for goods in a shop with a cheque, backed by a cheque card.

The shopkeeper pays in the cheque at the bank and receives the amount on the cheque from our bank account.

Why do we need trade? Trade supplies us with things which we are not able to produce ourselves. For centuries, merchants have bought and sold, transported and exchanged all kinds of goods all over the world. They went by sea, by river, crossed deserts and mountains.

Traders needed to move their goods as quickly and easily as possible. This is why roads and ports were built, and larger and larger boats were developed. Markets began to spring up at the major crossroads. The markets grew into towns, where traders and craftsmen came to live and to sell their goods. **The first great seafaring traders of the ancient western world were the Phoenicians*.** Their sturdy ships criss-crossed the Mediterranean Sea, bringing gold and ivory from Africa and lead and silver from Spain.

By the 13th century, the Italian merchants dominated trade with the East.

Their heavy sailing ships reached Venice and Genoa at the end of their long voyages with holds brimming with spices* and bales of silk. Deals were done as soon as the merchants reached the quayside. Prices were high, for silk and spices from the Far East were in great demand, and only Europe's wealthiest citizens and princes could afford them.

Gradually, European sailors ventured further and further on uncharted seas.

The Portuguese on board their caravels* sailed right round Africa to reach India and the Spice Islands. After Christopher Columbus had discovered America, the Spanish crossed the Atlantic, and returned laden with gold and silver.

In towns in the Middle Ages, merchants of the same trade would gather in covered halls built especially for them. There would be the cloth market, the corn exchange, the fish market and so on.

Foreign goods were appearing in Europe: coffee, tea, cocoa, sugar cane, potatoes. Merchants grew rich, and competed with each other to see which could finish a journey in the shortest time.

By the 17th century, the British and the Dutch had taken control of the trade route to India, and were bringing back diamonds and fine porcelain* from China.

Large towns need a constant supply of goods.

About a hundred and fifty years ago, at the time of the Industrial Revolution, towns were springing up fast around the first big factories. Thousands of peasants came from the country, looking for work.

How were these people to be clothed and fed?

Pedlars walked the streets with baskets of goods, but couldn't supply all their needs. Wholesale markets were needed.

Wholesale markets were open every day, and even at night.

Merchants and shopkeepers came to buy in bulk. They took meat, fish, vegetables and flowers back to their own shops to sell on to the people. Those days also saw the coming of larger stores – department stores. Customers could wander at ease from floor to floor. For the first time, prices were clearly marked on labels.

Entry was free, and you did not have to buy anything. Customers who did make a purchase could have their goods delivered by horse-drawn waggon, with posters on the side advertising the store.

By the 19th century, new forms of transport like trains and steam ships could move goods more quickly than ever before, but the horse and cart were still widely used.

<u>Trade has brought jobs to millions of people.</u>
Think how many people's hands any product passes through, between the time it is made and the time it is bought by the final customer – you, for instance. Nowadays, you find clementines, tomatoes and strawberries in the shops even in mid-winter. These fruits may have come from Morocco, Australia or Chile! Every day, refrigerated trucks, ships and cargo planes bring us fish and fresh fruit and vegetables.

<u>Advertising entices us to buy something!</u>
Glossy pictures in magazines, posters in the streets, mouth-watering images on our TV screens, are designed to persuade us to try a new washing powder or cream dessert. If you go into a supermarket, the choice is enormous. There are bargains to be had, the packets invite you to try their brand, all you need do is help yourself... how can you resist?

In some countries, a travelling salesman will cook you a pancake made with eggs from his own hens.

<u>The traditional way of selling things</u>
Shopping used to be a way of meeting people, chatting, exchanging news. Shopkeepers and stall holders would be your friends. Even today, in many countries buying and selling goes on as it always has done. Farmers and craftsmen in Africa and South America still sell their goods at local markets. In Europe too, especially in the country, supermarkets have not yet managed to wipe out the village stores or the local farm shop.

An open air market in South America

An African market under canvas

A shopping street in Far East Asia

A European supermarket

Trade led to the invention of weights and measures.

To barter or sell, you needed to have a fair idea of the weight, length and volume of the goods. People first started to use measurements thousands of years ago. To make a deal with your neighbour, it was important to know the size or weight of the goods you wanted to exchange. Since people could count, they have measured things by the span of a hand or a thumb's length. Feet or paces were useful for longer measurements.

In Egypt, fields were measured out using ropes 12 cubits long: a cubit was the distance from a man's fingertips to his elbow.

Desert peoples measured the distance between wells in terms of how far away you could hear a shout or shoot an arrow.

The foot is a very common unit of measurement – although not many people have feet twelve inches long!

Ancient Egyptian ruler

From early times, people have tried to set out a system of measurements that everyone can agree on.

To make trade and tax-collecting easier, kings in ancient times organised traders and farmers in their kingdoms to use the same measurements. Known as standard measurements, these gave a fixed value to the length of a foot or a cubit.

Both the Romans and the Egyptians used the palm of the hand as a unit of measurement: one palm measured about 7.5 cm.

Peasant farmers were not interested in the exact surface of a field, in any case; they preferred to measure it by the time it took to plough. In the Middle Ages, most products were measured in containers: they were sold by volume, not by weight. A merchant could cheat by not filling up his containers properly. He might buy a jar of grain full to the brim, and sell it on with an inch or two to spare at the top!

About 4,000 years ago, Egyptian peasants measured the harvest using a kind of barrel called a bushel. The measured grain was tipped into baskets and stored.

Wood is sold fastened together in blocks measuring one cubic metre.

Later, standard units were invented to check the containers used for measuring.

The standards had to be kept in a safe place. Even so, many were falsified and people were cheated. Worse still, measurements often varied between different regions, and different products. In Britain, for example, the bushel had different values in London and in Exeter, and a bushel of wheat was not equivalent to a bushel of oats.

There had to be a new way of measuring that was fair and common to all.

During the French Revolution at the end of the 18th century, scientists decided to find a measure which could not be altered, based on the Earth itself. The length of the meridian was divided by forty million and in 1799, after seven years of calculations, the metre was born!

In medieval markets, stone containers which could not be moved ensured a standard measure of grain.

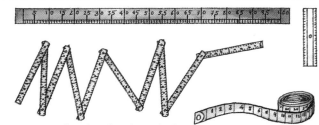

The metre is the basis of the international metric system.

It can be divided or multiplied by 10
1 metre = 10 decimetres
= 100 centimetres
1 kilometre = 1,000 metres

A litre is a measurement of volume.

It is the amount of liquid contained in a cube measuring ten centimetres on each side.
A kilogram is the weight of a litre of pure water at 0 degrees Centigrade.

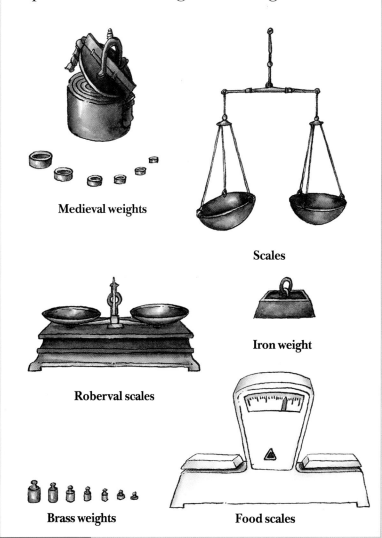

Medieval weights

Scales

Iron weight

Roberval scales

Brass weights

Food scales

Measuring led to writing. Quantities needed to be recorded. Writing was invented so that people in charge could keep accounts of taxes and harvests. It helped trade run smoothly.

The first writing was developed in Sumer, in Mesopotamia, in the Middle East, more than five thousand years ago.
To help them keep a check on offerings made at the temple, the priests who governed the city had the idea of using sharp sticks to mark off the number of flocks and harvests on tablets of soft clay.

This early writing is called cuneiform, meaning wedge-shaped.
It is made up of angles and wedge shapes arranged in different patterns. At first, it took the form of drawings representing the object, which we call pictograms. To write the word 'corn', you would draw an ear of grain. By putting two signs together, you could express a more complicated idea. For instance, a bullock's head placed next to a mountain would mean that the herds had come from the other side of the mountains. Even so, the scribes had a lot of symbols to learn. Writing would have to be simplified.
Next, the drawings became abstract.
Instead of standing for an object, they began to stand for sounds. We call these phonograms. To write 'idea', you would draw the symbols for an eye and for a deer. Six hundred symbols covered anything you wanted to express. Reading the writing was like unscrambling a riddle. It spread to neighbouring countries, but only the rich and powerful had the right to use it. Scribes learned their craft in the temple school, and soon became very powerful people in society.

Our alphabet comes from the Phoenicians, via the Greeks.

H. C. Rawlinson (1810-1895) working on an inscription engraved on a wall

The word 'hieroglyph' means 'writing of the gods' in Greek.

The beautiful writing of the Ancient Egyptians includes both pictograms and phonograms. It has been found carved into stone in temples and tombs. Scribes also wrote in ink on scrolls of papyrus, made from reeds which grew on the banks of the Nile. Papyrus stems were woven together, flattened and dried, to form sheets. Scribes used a quicker, more simple script than hieroglyphics, demotic script, for everyday matters. It read from right to left, rather like Arabic.

Champollion (1790-1832) grappled to uncover the secret of hieroglyphics for years, using his knowledge of other ancient languages. He succeeded, but died, exhausted, at only forty-two.

In 1824, a French scientist, Jean-François Champollion, managed to decipher Egyptian hieroglyphics, thanks to the Rosetta stone. The inscription carved on it was written in three ways: demotic script, hieroglyphics, and Greek. Champollion guessed it was the same text in three languages. His work has helped us learn about life in Egypt 4,000 years ago.
In 1846, a British diplomat, Henry Rawlinson, managed to understand the cuneiform script of the Sumerians.

Each letter of our western alphabet has its own sound.

By combining the twenty-six letters of our alphabet in every possible way, you can write down all the sounds of the European languages. Phoenician merchants invented this very practical system around 1,500 BC and used it to communicate with foreign traders. The Greeks improved the system by introducing vowels. The Greek alphabet was taken up by the Romans, who spread it throughout western Europe.

Some examples of Greek writing: it reads from left to right.

The Greeks had the idea of writing on animal skins.

Parchment owes its name to the town of Pergamum in present day Turkey, where it was first made. Sheep and calf skins were the best: they were cleaned, bleached, scraped and smoothed, and could then be used on both sides. They were folded and sewn together to make the first books in western history, called codices.

Rolled manuscripts gave way to bound books.

The Greeks introduced a new writing instrument: a reed pen, sharpened and slit down the middle to hold ink. Today's pens developed from this idea.

Writing became widely used and developed throughout the Roman Empire.

Engraved inscriptions appeared on stone monuments, praising the glory of the emperors. Scribes were often mere slaves. Lectors, or readers, dictated books for slaves to copy out. Messengers carried written despatches all over the Empire.

How Arabic figures gradually evolved

Literacy began among the privileged classes, but soon most of the Roman middle-classes knew how to read and write. The Empire was unified by a single, official language – Latin.

The figures we use as numbers have a very long history as well.

Throughout the Middle Ages, the Arabs recognised the importance of ancient learning and travelled widely between East and West. They brought us paper, invented by the Chinese much earlier, and introduced numbers, which probably came from India. Originally, figures were letters, which had been transformed over the years. A figure's position in a number alters its value: 12 is not the same as 21, and 123 is less than 312. It's an ingenious system!

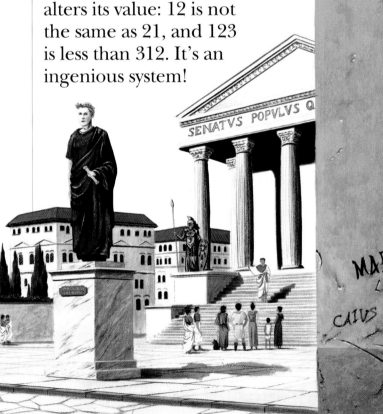

After the collapse of the Roman Empire in the 5th century, precious books were kept safe in monasteries, which had their own libraries. Here scribes, illuminators and painters all worked together to copy the ancient manuscripts, so that learning would not die out.

A faster and more legible writing was developed in Emperor Charlemagne's reign in the 8th century. Carolingian script was smaller, quicker, and looked more like today's writing. Monks and copyists wrote on parchment with pens made from goose or crow's feathers, sharpened to a point. Using fine, animal-hair brushes, they painted complex designs. The colours came from gold leaf, soot, and crushed insect eggs, mixed with gelatine or white of egg.

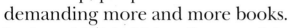

Movable metal type: letters were cast in metal and put together word by word, line by line, by the typesetter*.

The last stage: the sheet of paper is being pressed against letters covered with ink.

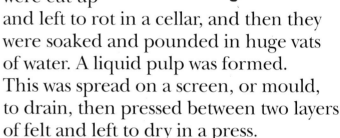

It took a lot of work and a long time to produce a book by hand. Books were rare and expensive. By the end of the Middle Ages, schools were beginning to develop; people were demanding more and more books.

In about 1447, in Mainz, Germany, Johannes Gutenberg invented a simple method to print books, using movable metal type.
He arranged letters made of lead on a metal plate, covered them with ink and pressed a sheet of paper against the metal. He could repeat this until he had printed all the copies he needed.

The art of printing could never have been developed if paper had not existed.
Paper was invented by the Chinese two thousand years ago. Old rags were cut up and left to rot in a cellar, and then they were soaked and pounded in huge vats of water. A liquid pulp was formed. This was spread on a screen, or mould, to drain, then pressed between two layers of felt and left to dry in a press.

It was not long before printing workshops sprang up everywhere.
First of all, they published Bibles and prayer books, Ancient Greek and Roman works and accounts of travels. New occupations developed: street hawkers sold books and rag-and-bone men collected scraps of material to make into paper.

A large proportion of the population was reading newspapers by the 19th century.

As printing methods grew faster, people had the idea of publishing single sheets of news for every day.

These were the first newspapers. They were called 'gazettes', from the Italian gazzetta, a small coin which was all that you needed to buy the paper. Gutenberg's hand-operated printing press was still used, but it could only print 300 sheets of paper a day. Printing had to improve.

Letter plates were replaced by rotary printing presses, with cylinders that turned.

The sheets of paper were drawn through rollers, and the ink flowed onto them automatically. But it still took too long to set the letters on the page. Then, in the 19th century, the linotype was invented. It could set complete lines of type in strips, and could typeset* 9,000 characters per hour. In 1846, in the USA, the first modern printing press produced 95,000 pages of newsprint in one hour!

But all these clever machines have not replaced handwriting!

Your writing is an expression of you. By writing, you can communicate in a direct and personal way with simple tools.

Can you think of peoples in the world who use writing different from ours?

In order to learn to read, you have to learn twenty-six different letters of the alphabet. Can you read French?

The Greek alphabet gave birth to the Cyrillic alphabet, which is used by many of the Slavonic peoples – Serbs and Russians for example.

Arabic is one of the Semitic languages. You read it from right to left.

Indian script is about two thousand years old. It probably developed from the Phoenician* alphabet in a different way to ours.

Chinese children have to learn thousands of different symbols, or characters. Each character is a different word.

The revolutionary invention that is the wheel

There is no such thing as a wheel in Nature. People did not just find it, as they had fire, they had to think up that round, rolling object which has become so important in so many aspects of our lives. It was an extraordinary invention, possibly the most important in the history of mankind.

Just think of life without wheels!

No cars, no carts even: to move something, however heavy, you would have to drag it or carry it on your back. To travel, you would have to walk. There would be no watches or clocks to tell the time, no bicycles or trains. Before the invention of the wheel, people managed to move enormous weights, like blocks of stone for building, by felling trees, and sliding the load over the logs, rather like rollers. A great feat of engineering, but it took a lot of effort, and many people.

We think the first wheels were made in Asia Minor in about 4,000 BC.

Fixed to a primitive cart, they helped people move quite substantial loads. Over the years, the heavy solid wooden wheels gradually developed into lighter ones with spokes. Then came the introduction of metal, and now our cars run on wheels protected by a cushion of air enclosed in a rubber tyre!

2,500 BC

1,000 BC

Europe, 1850

Modern tyre

A plough

The plough, which allowed farming to develop, was first invented without a wheel.

The earliest ploughs, dating from about 3,500 BC, did not have wheels but were just simple wooden blades. Wheeled ploughs were much more efficient. The animals did not have to strain so hard to pull them, so the furrows ran straighter and could be dug more quickly. The ploughs had a metal blade, called a ploughshare, which sank into the soil and dug the furrows, and an angled mouldboard, which turned the earth to one side. Soil that has been well tilled and aired produces a good harvest. The farmers would take their grain to the mill. But how would the mill turn, if the wheel had not been invented?

Wheels which make other wheels turn

The knife-grinder sharpens knives on his grindstone.

A spinning wheel to spin wool into yarn

You turn a wheel to work the pulley on a well.

The Middle Ages saw the introduction of many new machines that need more than one wheel to make them work: windmills, watermills, spinning-wheels, clocks...

The movement of one wheel is transferred to another, either through a flexible link, a drive belt made of leather, or because each wheel has teeth, or cogs, which fit into one another. These cogwheels are gears and they can make the machine speed up or slow down.

In paper mills, forges*, tanneries and sawmills, watermills harnessed energy from water.

How were sturdy medieval cartwheels made?

The central piece, the hub, was often carved from elm. The spokes were made of oak. One end of each spoke was fixed in the hub, the other in the rim, which was made of curved pieces of wood fitted together. The outside of the rim was bound with iron to strengthen it.

Wheels transform a jerky back-and-forth movement into a smooth, circular motion.

By working a pedal with his foot, a knife-grinder drove a crank* to turn his grindstone. In forges or paper-mills, wooden cams* were fixed to the wheels. Each time the wheel turned, the cams would lift hammers which in turn beat the metal or paper pulp. Even today, engines work on the principle of cranks and cams.

A treadmill can be used to lift heavy loads high in the air. A man can make it turn.

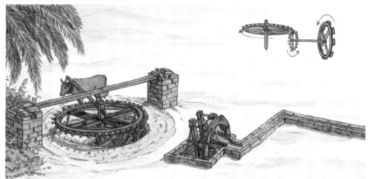

A chain pump is used to draw water. An animal turns a cogwheel, which drives another wheel fitted with buckets.

In a windmill, a system of gears transfers the movement of the sails to the grindstone, which grinds the grain into flour.

A 19th-century treadmill: the man is driving the wheel round by climbing on the rungs. The rope winds up, dragging the blocks of stone along.

The hey-day of the stage-coach

If you were to walk from York to London, it would take you over a week.
In a modern train, you could do it in two hours.
The same journey, in the mid 19th century, by stage-coach, used to take two days.
The stage-coach was suspended by leather thongs from a framework on wheels called a chassis. This suspension made it less bumpy to ride in and easier to pull.
Stages were set up every ten miles for mail coaches.
The coachman would change horses for the next leg of the journey; passengers could rest and have something to eat. You can still see some of the old coaching inns by the side of main roads. Coaches ran regularly to most principal towns.
Fierce rivalry between companies led to fast, punctual services and often breakneck races to reach a stage ahead of a rival coach!

From winding paths to paved roads

The first roads were made of earth. Then after the invention of the wheel, roads had to be harder and straighter. The Romans were the first to build networks of paved roads. Some modern roads still follow the straight lines of Roman roads.

McAdam's invention

John McAdam, an 18th-century Scottish engineer, realised that the foundations of a road carry the weight of traffic, so they need to be compressed and kept dry. If they are not, the surface becomes pitted and sunken. He constructed roads with a curved surface so water would run off them, and covered the base with several layers of small stones. Later, in the 19th century, road-makers began to cover the surface with black tar. Modern roads are sometimes surfaced with concrete.

Two wheels, one behind the other: here comes the bicycle!

The first bicycle was invented in Paris in 1791. It had two wheels, but you sat on one and pushed yourself along with your feet! Later, two pedals and a crank were fixed directly to the front wheel hub. The pedalling movement was transferred through the crank to turn the wheel.

The bigger the wheels, the faster the cyclist could go! Finally, the wheels were made of equal size, with the pedals placed between them with a rear chain drive. And that's how your bicycle works!

Penny-farthing bicycle

Bicycle with rear chain drive

Racing bike with gears

Ten man tandem!

Steam becomes a source of energy.

After Papin's famous steam boiler, another Frenchman, Joseph Cugnot, invented the first three wheeled steam car in 1769.

The 18th century saw a revolutionary new invention: a machine powered by steam.

It was capable of pumping water, driving a hammer in a forge* and making wheels turn. The French engineer Denis Papin (1647-1712) first had the idea of using the power of steam. Thomas Newcomen, from Dartmouth, was the first to develop an efficient steam engine which was to play a major part in the Industrial Revolution.

When water boils, it turns into steam. It is possible to confine the steam in a boiler, and then let it escape under pressure through a valve*, just as it does in a pressure cooker. This force can then be harnessed.

The power of steam transformed life.

It was used down mines and in factories to drive machinery and move heavy loads. At the beginning of the 19th century came the first attempts at running an engine on rails. Steam locomotives burned huge quantities of coal or wood, which heated a boiler full of water.

A jointed connecting-rod transforms the up-and-down movement of pistons into the circular movement of wheels.

Connecting-rod
Piston
Cylinder

Portable steam engines and traction engines started to replace man and animal power.

How does a steam engine move?

The steam pushes a closely fitting metal rod called a piston in a cylinder. Then a valve shuts off the steam: the pressure drops, allowing the piston to come back again. The connecting-rods transfer the up-and-down movement of the pistons to the wheels, and the engine moves forward.

By the beginning of the 19th century, the first steam locomotives were appearing in Europe, mainly as fairground attractions.

George Stephenson (1781-1848), a British engineer, is often called 'the Father of the Railway'. He built the world's first public railway for steam trains in 1825: it ran from Stockton to Darlington. His famous Rocket locomotive won a prize in 1829 for the best designed steam engine. It could travel 47 k.p.h., faster than a horse could gallop.

One of the earliest trains. The carriages were simply stage-coaches set on rails. Coach makers were the first carriage makers.

Because the British were the first to develop the railway system, trains all over the world still drive on the left.

Before long, railways were spreading across the countryside.

At first, they only ran between the big cities, but soon the network spread, connecting smaller towns and even villages. People would turn out on a Sunday to watch the train go by! Many men were employed to keep the trains running: engine drivers, stokers to feed the fires with coal, signalmen to guide the trains and lamp-lighters to light up the rails. A steam locomotive would use ten kilograms of coal and 100 litres of water for every kilometre it travelled. The tender was coupled behind the engine and carried the six tonnes of coal and 40,000 litres of water that the engine would use!

How is a railway track built?

First the track is spread with ballast, a bed of granite chips to deaden vibration of the rails. Then the sleepers are laid over the top: once they were made of wood, but now they are made from reinforced concrete. They keep the rails really firm.

The first crossing of the continent of the United States of America by train took place on 15th May 1869.

The gauge* is 1.435 metres in most European countries. Finally, the steel rails are fixed to the sleepers. On an express line, they are welded together to cut down on jolts and noise.

A train's engine is very powerful.

It can pull all kinds of trucks which may carry grain, or new cars, or deep-frozen products in enormous refrigerated containers.

Steam train, around 1920

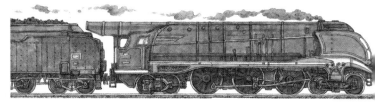

Most trains nowadays run on electricity, just as trams and underground trains do. The power is sent through a live 'third' rail, the conductor rail, where it is picked up by the train's 'collector shoes'. Some electric trains, such as inter-city trains, pick up electricity from an overhead cable and a pantograph fixed on the roof of the engine. Other trains have diesel engines.

The train driver has to obey the coloured signal lights.

To avoid accidents, the track is divided into sections. Once one train has started its journey onto a section, a red signal lights up and the train behind must wait until the line is clear.

Trains running through several countries cover great distances. They pull sleeping-cars, where passengers can bed down for the night, dining-cars and sometimes recreation cars where children can play. Around 1900 the Trans-Siberian ran from Paris to Vladivostok, a port on the far east coast of Siberia. Some of its coaches were very luxurious, but if you could not afford that, you could travel third class on wooden seats. The most prestigious train of them all was the Orient Express, linking Paris and Ostend with Constantinople. In Australia you can go 3,840 kms, from Perth to Sydney, on some of the straightest track in the world. And soon you will be able to go by train underneath the English Channel!

On mountainous routes, where the gradient is steepest, the rack railway was the answer. The trains have a cogwheel which catches onto teeth in a third central rail. The highest railway in the world is in Peru, in the Andes. The rails are built in a zig-zag, and the train has one engine in front and one behind.

In the 19th century, the best craftsmen used luxury furnishings to create carriages for important people. Queen Victoria enjoyed travelling by train and slept better in her sleeping-car than she did in her royal palaces at Balmoral and Windsor!

The fastest train in the world is the French TGV. It can reach a speed of 500 k.p.h.

This overground urban train is fully automatic. It has no driver, and is controlled by computer.

Marshalling yard for goods

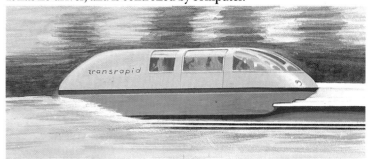

This experimental train, 'Maglev', is kept in the air by electric magnets, so there is no friction on the rails. It is in service in Japan.

The internal combustion engine led to the invention of the automobile.

During the first car race, between Paris and Rouen in France in July 1894, the winner reached an average speed of between 17 and 20 k.p.h.!

The earliest cars were called automobiles.

The word means a vehicle that moves by itself. The internal combustion engine, patented in 1862, was built into a car in 1864. Karl Benz invented a three-wheeled car in 1885. By 1893 the car had four wheels, and in 1895, F.W. Lanchester, an Englishman, introduced pneumatic tyres and reverse gear. The modern car was born! But, without protection from roof or windscreen, drivers got soaked if it rained! The cars often broke down and their drivers had to double as mechanics.

Articulated lorry
(38 tonnes)

19th-century
steam-
powered
lorry
(5 tonnes)

The first bus, built
in 1885, carried
eight passengers.

A modern bus

To fuel a steam-driven machine, you needed to carry water, and wood or coal on board. It was a cumbersome business! Most modern engines are internal combustion engines. Much more practical, they run on petrol or diesel, which are both products of oil.

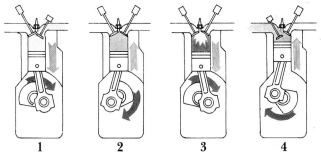

1   2   3   4

What happens inside the engine of a car?

There are four hollow tubes called cylinders. Inside each one there is a piston. This is how a four-stroke engine works:

1. The piston goes down, drawing in a mixture of petrol and air.
2. The piston goes up again, compressing the mixture.
3. The spark plug ignites a spark, which makes the petrol explode, forcing the piston down.
4. After the explosion, the piston rises, forcing out the waste gas products.

Most engines are four-stroke engines: they have four cylinders and four spark-plugs. A petrol engine does not burn up all its fuel. It forces the waste products, including a dangerous gas called carbon monoxide, out through the exhaust box and into the atmosphere.

Racing cars have very wide tyres. This helps the car grip the track and keeps it more stable.

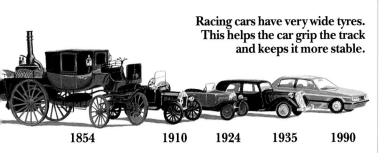

1854   1910   1924   1935   1990

Boats were invented thousands of years ago.

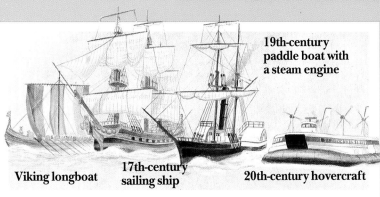

19th-century paddle boat with a steam engine

Viking longboat

17th-century sailing ship

20th-century hovercraft

Boats are known to have been used in Mesopotamia before 4,000 BC.

Early boats were hollowed-out tree trunks. A plank of wood served as a paddle to propel the boat. But rowing was hard work – there was no animal that could be trained to do it! From ancient times up to the 16th century, slaves or prisoners were forced to wield the banks of oars

A Roman ship with a wheel rudder on the starboard* side.

on heavy ships called galleys.

On longer sea voyages, the wind's force was used as well. A simple piece of cloth was hoisted to the mast to catch the wind: the sail had been invented!

The sail was a very clever invention!

The helmsman's wheel turns the afterpiece of the rudder, a wide, flat piece of wood or steel.

As the wind blows, it fills the sails and pushes the boat forwards. People first made use of this discovery about 5,000 BC. Early sails were square. Then people living round the Mediterranean invented triangular sails: they could sail against the wind and manoeuvre the boat more easily.

How does a boat stay afloat?

It does not sink because it is hollow, even though it is very heavy. Its weight is distributed widely over the water, and a balance is maintained between the air inside the keel and the water around it.

What is a rudder?

It is a flat piece of wood or metal fixed to the back, or stern, of a ship below the water. It is linked to a bar called a tiller, or a wheel. As a sailor moves the wheel or the tiller, the angle of the rudder alters and the ship changes direction.

The great working sailing ships are long gone.
Their names still have a romantic ring: barks, brigs, schooners and clippers, they were huge ships with three or four masts. Built of wood and hard-wearing, each ship was suited to its task, such as fishing or transporting goods. Almost 200 years ago, the largest ships began to be built with engines instead of sails. The engine drove a paddle-wheel, the paddles working like little oars to drive the ship along. In 1836 the propeller engine was invented.

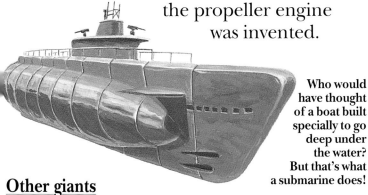

Who would have thought of a boat built specially to go deep under the water? But that's what a submarine does!

Other giants appeared: ocean liners.
At the beginning of the century, the *Mauretania*'s powerful engines enabled her to cross the Atlantic in just five days. Have you heard of the *Titanic*, which claimed to be unsinkable, but which went down on her first voyage in 1912? These grand old liners were like cities. They carried over a thousand passengers, and hundreds of cooks, waiters and cabin staff to look after the passengers. The last of the Atlantic liners, *Queen Elizabeth II* was launched in 1968.

Nowadays, even the largest ships can be handled by only a dozen men.
They maintain radio contact with land, and they are kept informed of their exact position in the ocean by satellite. They use radar to locate other vessels and find out the depth of the water. An automatic pilot has taken over from a man at the helm.

A paddle-boat taking passengers and goods up the Mississippi river in America in the 19th century

Huge propellers drive the ship forward by pushing water back. They are connected to the rudder.

Container ships

Tanker, built to carry minerals such as oil

Most ships today are built of steel.

The hot air balloon invented by the Montgolfier brothers, in France, in 1783

The first flying machines looked more like bats than birds!

For a long time, people had dreamt of flying. At the turn of the century, conquering the air seemed more and more possible. Men pursued the sport of flying enthusiastically, risking their lives in unstable contraptions made of canvas and wood, and held together by wire.

In 1890, Clément Ader achieved the first powered take-off.

His flying machine, named Eole (Greek for wind), left the ground for several metres. In 1903, the American Wright brothers made the first historic flight in a small plane with propellers. In 1909, Louis Blériot crossed the Channel from France.

Airships are balloons that you can steer. In 1919, the Zeppelin crossed the Atlantic.

Then in 1927, Charles Lindbergh, an American, made the first non-stop crossing of the Atlantic in 33.5 hours.

Aeroplane built by the Wright brothers

The early aircraft were mostly used for carrying mail.

The Douglas 'DC-3', the first modern civilian airliner, was launched in 1936.

It could carry 21 passengers. Twenty years later, airliners had developed into giants like the Boeing '707' which can carry 184 passengers.

There's a highway code in the air as well as on the road!

To avoid accidents, aircraft travel in air corridors. If two aircraft are using the same corridor, they have to leave a space of at least six hundred metres high between them. Before take off, the pilots make a plan of the flight: they choose the route they will follow depending on the weather reports, the distance they have to go and the altitude of the flight. All aircraft are tracked from the ground by radio or radar.

Clément Ader's first flight

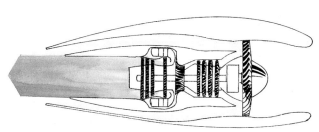

The Canari bird, 1929   Boeing 727

Microlight

Helicopter

Light aeroplane
with propellers

By shooting the air out from behind, the turbofan propels the aircraft forwards.

How does an aeroplane fly?

Its speed and the shape of its wings keep it in the air. The air flowing over the top of the wing travels faster than the air flowing underneath. This causes a difference in pressure above and below the wing and gives the plane lift. At take-off, the pilot turns the wings into the wind to give the plane added lift. Although the planes are big, they have to be very light, so they are often built of aluminium*. Until the 1950s, aircraft were fitted with combustion engines, (like cars), which drove propellers, but the fastest they could fly was 700 k.p.h. Nowadays, they are built with turbojets.

Jet aircraft need a long runway for take-off and landing. Some airports are too small, and light aircraft with propellers still perform a valuable service in many parts of the world, especially where roads are scarce.

Helicopters have blades which spin at a high speed, instead of wings.
They can rarely travel faster than 300 k.p.h., but they can land almost anywhere: on a mountain, or in a clearing or on the roof of a building.

Jet aircraft have very powerful engines.

The turbojet sucks in the cold air, heats it up by burning fuel, then shoots it out from the back at enormous speed. This leaves the white vapour trail you may sometimes see in the sky.

Helicopters can fly very low, and even hover. They are used for keeping an eye on roads and forests, for transporting injured people from awkward places to hospital and as luxury taxis for those who can afford them!

Measuring the world

It was only two centuries ago that people learned how to measure long distances and pinpoint precise positions around the globe. Complicated instruments and difficult mathematics are needed to make these calculations with accuracy.

How to find out where on Earth you are!

As the Earth rotates on its axis, different countries receive the sun's light one after another. When the sun rises in Europe, it is night in America and midday in India.

To measure speed, sailors used a knotted rope trailing behind the boat. They counted knots as sand ran through the hour-glass.

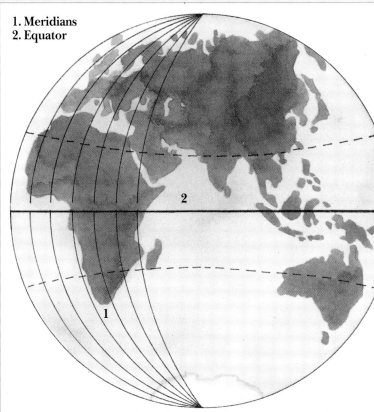

1. Meridians
2. Equator

The meridians are imaginary lines around the Earth connecting the North Pole to the South Pole. The Paris meridian was used to calculate the metre.

Scientists divide the world into time-zones marked out by the meridians. The most famous meridian, the Greenwich Meridian, passes through London. To work out their position at sea, sailors calculate the longitude* and latitude*, their position east or west of the Greenwich Meridian, and north or south of the Equator, another imaginary line circling the Earth half-way between the two Poles. To find out latitude, navigators measure the angle between the sun and the horizon – since the angle varies according to where you are on Earth, they can get an accurate position.

An astronomical clock shows the movement of the planets.

Telling the passing hours

The nocturlabe, like the astrolabe, is an old-fashioned instrument which tells the time by measuring the height of the stars above the horizon.

Our ancestors used to measure time by the passing of the seasons, and by the rising, progression and setting of the sun.

By observing stars in the night sky, astronomers in ancient times divided the day into 12 hours and the year into 360 days. We now know that it takes the Earth 24 hours to make a complete turn on its axis, and 365 days and 6 hours to make a full circuit of the sun. To make up those extra 6 hours into a full day, we have 366 days in every fourth, or leap, year.

For sports competitions, a stopwatch can measure time to one hundredth of a second.

What time is it?

People in the ancient world used to tell the time with sun-dials, sand-timers and water-clocks. The first mechanical clocks were invented in the Middle Ages; the regular swinging of a weight to the end of a pendulum turned the hands. Later, the pendulum was replaced by a spring which slowly unwound. When you wind a watch or clock, you are winding the spring up again. Quartz clocks and watches use an electric battery which sets a quartz crystal vibrating. Atomic clocks are so accurate that they only lose one second every 3,000 years! They are used to set the international standard for a second.

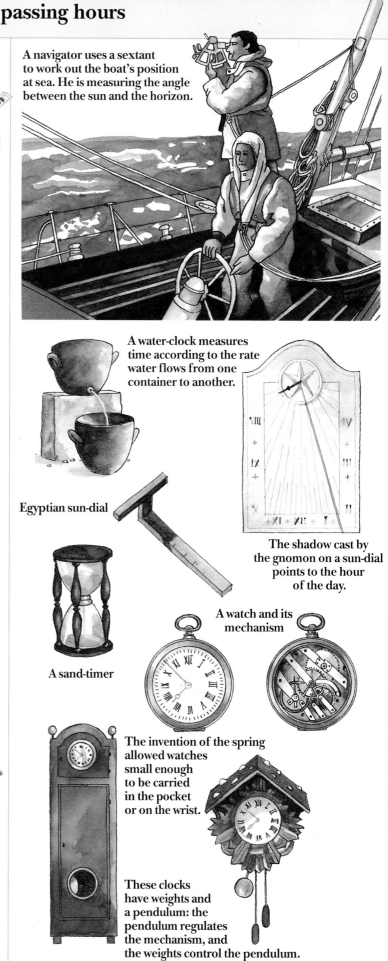

A navigator uses a sextant to work out the boat's position at sea. He is measuring the angle between the sun and the horizon.

A water-clock measures time according to the rate water flows from one container to another.

Egyptian sun-dial

The shadow cast by the gnomon on a sun-dial points to the hour of the day.

A watch and its mechanism

A sand-timer

The invention of the spring allowed watches small enough to be carried in the pocket or on the wrist.

These clocks have weights and a pendulum: the pendulum regulates the mechanism, and the weights control the pendulum.

Think of all the things you do when you get up first thing in the morning. You get out of bed, put on the light, wash, make and eat breakfast, go to school by foot or bus, bike or car. From the moment you open your eyes you are using electricity, gas, petrol...and your own muscles. You are using energy all the time!

Energy comes from the Greek word 'energeia' which means 'power in action'. In science, we say that a body, or a system, has energy if it is capable of doing work, in other words, transferring power.

When a horse uses all its strength to pull a plough, it is working and using energy. When you pedal your bike to make it go fast, you are using some of the energy you stored in your body when you had breakfast. Every second of the day, people are using energy.
The search for sources of energy, as well as ways to conserve what we already have, is one of the most important concerns of our modern society.

There are many different forms of energy: mechanical, electrical, chemical, thermal, nuclear... You can transform one form of energy into another. A battery transforms chemical energy into electrical energy, and a steam engine transforms thermal energy into mechanical energy.

All these harness, produce or transform energy:
1. Dam - 2. Solar panels - 3. Uranium mine
4. Nuclear power station - 5. Windmill
6. Hydroelectric power station built on a river (using the energy produced by water) 7. Coal mine - 8. Tidal power station*
9. Oil rig - 10. Oil refinery - 11. Power plant making gas from coal - 12. Forestry - 13. Organic farm waste used to produce methane gas. - 14. House with solar panels.

Electricity was not mastered until the 19th century.

Before houses had electricity, people used individual lamps, lit by candles, oil or gas.

Electricity: it is so easy for us to use that we take it for granted.

Obtaining light or heat at the flick of a switch would have seemed like magic to our ancestors. Even so, we know that the first experiments with electricity were made a very long time ago. About 2,500 years ago, the Greek philosopher and scientist Thales of Miletus found he could cause sparks if he rubbed some amber* with a piece of cloth. Thales had discovered static electricity. But it was many centuries before anyone discovered how to produce and make use of an electric current or an electric generator.

What makes electricity work?

When an electric current passes along a wire, millions of minute particles, called electrons, move about, colliding with the atoms which make up the metallic wire. As the atoms are disturbed, they release energy in the form of heat or light. The quantity of heat or light produced is proportional to the resistance of the conducting wire: in other words, the more the atoms resist as the electrons move along, the greater the heat that is produced. Certain things, like wood or glass, do not conduct electricity at all. Others, like iron and many other metals, are conductors, but they are resistant. The filament in an electric bulb works on this principle: it is made of tungsten, a metal which offers great resistance, so it gets hotter and hotter until it glows white and produces light.

Volta's battery

Alessandro Volta demonstrating his electric battery to a group of scientists in 1800, in the presence of the French Emperor Napoleon.

Electricity: magic for everyone!

Thomas Edison lit up the world when he invented electric light.

You can read on a light bulb how powerful it is. A one hundred watt* bulb is brighter than one of twenty-five watts. In Britain, domestic appliances run on between 200 and 250 volts. Volts are the electrical pressure which pushes an electric current round a circuit*. The name comes from the Italian physicist, Alessandro Volta, who invented the first electric battery in 1794.

The first electric light bulb was invented by Thomas Edison. The lack of oxygen in the bulb allows the wire filament to heat up and glow white hot, without burning.

The first battery

Volta's battery was made from a series of silver discs separated from one another by wads of cloth soaked in salt water. Nowadays, batteries aren't quite so big! You can move them around quite easily.

You can produce electricity yourself!

Does the headlamp on your bike work without a battery? As you pedal, a dynamo transforms your energy into electric energy amd produces a current to power your headlamp. Inside the dynamo, there is a magnet and an electric circuit, connected to the wheel as it turns.

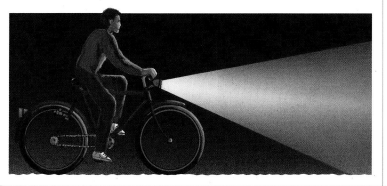

Car batteries are storage batteries; they can be recharged by the car's engine as it moves.

Providing electricity for a whole country

During the last century, electric power stations were fuelled by coal. As the coal burned, it heated water which turned into steam. The steam was used to drive turbines which generated electricity...just like the dynamo on your bicycle!

In 1882, Edison lit up the city of New York with electric light from his coal-fired electric power station.

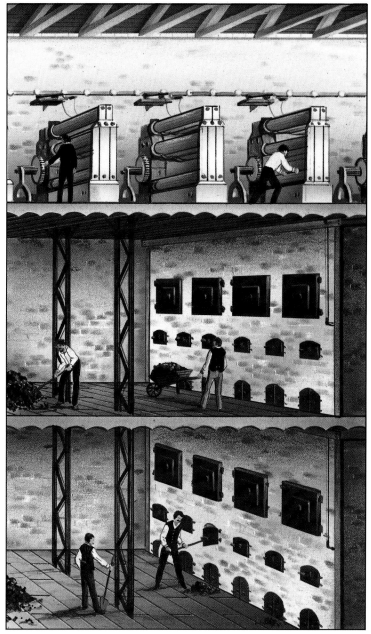

Fossil fuels: coal and oil

During the 19th century, Europe became industrialised: it based its development on the use of coal as fuel. At that time, it was the main source of energy. It was used in many different ways: to drive steam engines, to produce electricity and to smelt iron for the steel needed for building the new machines.

What is coal?
Coal is formed from the remains of trees and giant ferns which grew on Earth about 250 million years ago. It is a fossil*. Away from the air, the vegetation of rivers and swamps rotted and gradually turned into carbon. There are different types of coal. Those compressed for longest, such as anthracite, are rich in carbon and are the better quality coals.
Lignite and peat are softer and contain less carbon, and they do not burn so well.

Where is it found?
Since the Middle Ages, people have mined* coal in open-cast mines. Later, they learnt how to dig tunnels deep into the earth, looking for seams of coal. Mining has always been dangerous, laborious work. Until recently, hundreds of thousands of men were employed as miners in the British Coal industry.

Petroleum: treasure from under the ground
Today, stocks of coal in many pits have been exhausted; others are no longer considered financially viable and have been closed down. Petroleum has taken over from coal. The name means 'oil from rock' – it looks like a thick greenish brown oil and it springs out of the ground.

What is petroleum?
Its other name is crude oil. Like coal, it is formed from organic material. Over millions of years, plants and animals died and drifted to the sea-bottom. Layers of soil gathered over the sludge, and pockets of it were trapped between layers of rock. Time and pressure turned the sludge into oil. Deep wells are dug to extract oil from under the ground. The first commercial oil-field was opened up in 1859 in Pennsylvania in America. Not all countries have their own oil-fields. Those that do not have to import their petroleum – it can travel huge distances.

First, oil is transported in huge pipes to the sea...

...where it is loaded onto giant oil tankers...

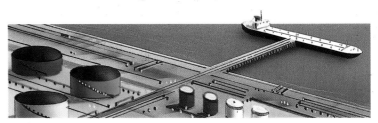

...which transport it to large industrial ports.

Gas and water drive our power stations.

High tension cables (400,000 volts), carry electricity from the power stations to the cities where it is needed.

They are then divided into lower tension cables (11,000 volts), which carry the electricity to individual houses at between 200 and 250 volts.

Other sources of energy from underground

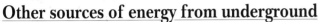

Butane and propane gas are present in the sub-soil*. We call them natural gases, to distinguish them from industrial gases. Gas burns, so we most often use it for heating and cooking, but it can be used for lighting as well. Neon lights in advertisements are powered by gas, as is krypton lighting. Like oil, gas is transported in giant pipelines.

A clean form of energy

Water power can also produce electricity. The force of the water as it spills from the top of the dam is used to drive the turbines.

Environmentalists* urge governments to make more use of water power, which is far cleaner than oil, and a better use of the Earth's resources.

A dam

Petroleum is purified in huge oil refineries ready for its different uses.

Tanker lorries transport it to a point of sale...

... a petrol station, for example.

49

An atom: electrons spinning around a central nucleus

The industrialised nations of the world are demanding more and more energy.

We double the amount of electricity we use every ten years. In Britain today, 20% of electricity is produced by nuclear power stations.

The heart of the matter

Nuclear comes from the Latin word nucleus, meaning core. All matter is made up of atoms, each with a nucleus. To produce energy, nuclear power stations use atoms from metals such as uranium 235 and plutonium. Splitting the nucleii of these atoms into two produces a great heat. This heat brings water to boiling point, and the steam drives turbines, just as in a coal-fired power station. But one gram of uranium 235 produces as much energy as 2 or 3 tonnes of coal! It is by far the most concentrated source of energy used by mankind.

Symbol warning danger from nuclear radiation

The dangers of nuclear energy

Using uranium and plutonium to create nuclear power produces radioactive waste: the waste products contain rays which are very dangerous. Depending on the level of radioactivity in these rays, living things exposed to them may die or become very ill. Nuclear waste remains dangerous for thousands of years, so what can we do with it? If we continue to dump it underground, are we just storing the problem for our children? Dangerous substances could leak out and return to the surface. Environmentalists* believe that it may be better to keep the waste in specially designed stores above ground, so that it can be regularly checked by scientists.

Cut-away diagram of a nuclear reactor: on the left, in red, is the atomic pile, which heats the water of the primary circuit (coloured orange). The primary circuit heats the water in the secondary circuit (yellow), turning it to steam. The steam drives an alternator which produces electricity.

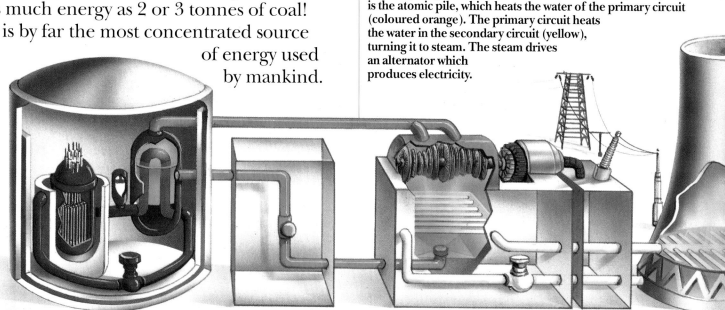

The sun: a source of energy that can never be used up

Clean energy, green power

We could make better use of the forces of Nature to provide energy in ways less harmful to the environment. We do not have to use up irreplaceable resources. The power of the sea can be harnessed in tidal power stations* to produce electricity. In certain parts of the world, natural hot springs of water or steam, called geysers, jet up into the air. In Iceland, geysers supply domestic heating and enable people to grow a variety of fruit and vegetables, even though the weather is very cold.

Solar energy

In Northern Europe during the cold winter months, vegetables can be grown in greenhouses, where large panes of glass let in plenty of sunlight. Sunlight warms the soil, which absorbs and then re-emits infrared rays. The glass traps the rays, which in turn keep the temperature inside the greenhouse warm. If the Earth only received a tiny amount of the sun's rays, this part would still represent 10,000 times more energy than we need. The problem is, how do we collect it and use it?

This telephone is powered by sunlight.

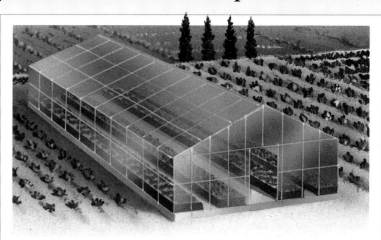

Nowadays solar power gives us heat.

The sun's rays are being used to heat some houses in the same way as they do greenhouses. Solar collectors on dark, heat-absorbent metallic plates heat up rather like the soil in a greenhouse. Once it has been trapped, the heat either warms the air directly, or heats a circuit of water which feeds the radiators – solar central heating!

Solar power turned into electricity

The sun's light energy can also be turned directly into electricity using photovoltaic cells*. This form of energy is used by heavy industry. Europe's biggest solar energy plant is at Themis in France.

A house with solar heating. It is fitted with panels of photoelectric cells*. Sloping panels can receive up to 10% more solar energy than vertical ones.

Did you know that light is made up of colours?

Isaac Newton made a hole in his shutter and found that white sunlight breaks down into different coloured lights.

Light that reaches us from the sun appears white, or rather transparent. In fact, it is a combination of an infinite number of coloured lights. In 1666, the English physicist Isaac Newton made sunlight pass through a prism, a little glass pyramid, and showed that white light is made up of colours: these are the seven colours of the rainbow.

In fact, there are many more than seven and they graduate from violet through to red. Beyond these two extremes, there are other colours which our eyes cannot see.

Before electric light, people used candles made of animal fat or wax. The light they shed was weak and orange-coloured.

In the triangle are the 3 primary colours. Round the circle are the 3 complementary colours, made from mixing 2 primary colours.

Light is in fact a wave.

When it hits anything that is not transparent, part of it is absorbed and part of it is reflected. If we think an object is yellow, it's because it reflects the yellow light and absorbs the other colours. If it looks red, it's because it is only reflecting red light, and so on. This discovery led scientists to believe that light is made up of waves, rather like ripples on the surface of water. The colour waves vary in shape – some are sharper than others. Red has the lowest pitch and the longest wavelength*, and violet the most acute pitch and the shortest wavelength.

Heat is the source of light.

When any substance is heated, it glows and becomes luminous once its temperature has reached 500 degrees.

As its temperature rises to 1,000 degrees, its colour will gradually change from deep red to a red that is almost white. Until Thomas Edison invented the electric light bulb in 1880, people did not have bright light. They only knew the gentle glow from burning oil and resin, candles made of animal fat or wax, then later, spirit or gas lamps.

The filament, the thread, in early electric light bulbs was heated to 2,800 degrees by an electric current.

Nowadays, the filament in a halogen lamp reaches 4,000 degrees. It can stand such a very high temperature because it is bathed in a gas called halogen.

Glass would shatter at this heat, so the bulb itself is made of quartz instead.

Coloured lights from burning powders!

Certain powders can colour flame.
The colour of a light does not always depend on the temperature of the thing that is burning. For example, if you throw certain powdered substances into the very hot flame of a gas-ring or a blow-lamp, they will glow brightly and colour the flame for a moment.

The art of making fireworks is called pyrotechnics.
A firework is made of two cartridges: one is filled with gunpowder, to launch the rocket into the air and to set light to the other cartridge, the one which produces brilliant flames of different colours. This second case is filled with a mixture of substances that will burn and different powders: zinc, copper powder for the blues and greens, sodium for the yellows, and so on. Fireworks must always be used with great care. They provide a lovely display for a celebration!

Moving pictures: the birth of cinema!

In a praxinoscope, images reflect off mirrors and appear to move.

Photography, cinema and television are part of our daily lives. They have all been invented since the early 19th century, and each one makes use of light.

The birth of photography.
Certain substances, such as silver chloride and Judean bitumen, turn more or less solid black under the effect of light.

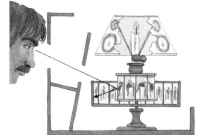 

People had realised this for a long time, but it was in 1827 that the French physicist Nicephore Niepce put the knowledge to work and produced photographs. He covered a pewter plate with bitumen and exposed it in a camera. Where light fell on it, the bitumen turned hard and black. Softer areas were then washed away, leaving a well-defined image.

This process was perfected in 1838 by Niepce's associate, Jacques Daguerre. His photographic images, known as daguerrotypes, soon became very popular for portraits.

In 1859, the British physicist James Maxwell took the first colour photograph.

The way was opened to cinematography.
Since 1852, scientists had been able to break down movement photographically into a sequence of still images. Many years before the cinema, people knew how to project these images through the 'magic lantern'. Then instruments like the praxinoscope made it possible to put the movement back together again. When images are shown rapidly enough one after another, your eyes hold the image they have just seen for a fraction of a second, even though the following image has already appeared. This is the principle of animation. The Lumière brothers put all these inventions together and gave us the cinema. They held their first public viewing in 1895.

Pictures you see on television consist of tiny points of light which move about on the screen.
The closer together the points of light, the more clear-cut the image; and the quicker they move about, the steadier the picture. The pictures on TV come from patterns of light which arrange and re-arrange themselves fifty times a second! All variations of colour come from different combinations of just three series of luminous dots: red, blue and green.

What is a laser beam?
Lasers are made from very pure, concentrated light. They emit beams so intense that they can travel great distances without growing dim or fading away. Astronomers direct beams onto small mirrors placed on the Moon, and then wait for them to 'bounce back'. Light travels at a certain speed, so scientists know that Earth is 380,000 kms away! Even greater distances can be calculated in light years, or the distance light travels in one year.

The pictures you see in this book are all made up of just four colours: black, blue (cyan), red (magenta), and yellow, each reproduced on a plate. When the printer puts the four images on top of one another, they form pictures like those in this book.

Lasers are used in colour printing, to reproduce full-colour pictures.
The scanner's photoelectric eye moves over a picture to analyse it. It sorts out the colours, and relays information to the laser so film can be produced for the printer.

Outer space is getting closer!

Sputnik, the first artificial satellite, launched in 1957

If you travel a distance of 80 kilometres into the sky, you will find yourself in the emptiness of space, far above the atmosphere where you can breathe.

Before Man could go into space, rockets had to be invented.

Only a rocket can reach the colossal speed of 28,000 k.p.h. required to overcome gravity.

A century lies between the writer Jules Verne's dream of a cannon-ball rocket and the huge Saturn V that sent spacecraft to the Moon.

A rocket needs no air: it takes its own oxygen supply to burn its fuel. The thrust of the first few minutes carries the rocket rapidly up into space.

The first real rocket was launched in 1926 by the American Robert Goddard.

'One small step for man, one giant step for Mankind'

So much preparation goes into sending a man into space. It takes years!

You have to build a spaceship with everything the passengers will need for their journey: air, water, food and fuel. The spaceship must be capable of returning to Earth later.

To leave its orbit and re-enter Earth's atmosphere, it brakes, then uses the air's friction to slow its speed from 28,000 k.p.h. to zero! This incredible braking mechanism ends with a parachute-assisted landing. One tiny error, and the spaceship will burn up. The Soviet astronaut Yuri Gagarin was the first human being to orbit* Earth. It took 108 minutes on 12th April, 1961. John Glenn was the first American astronaut: he completed an orbit in February 1962.

Men on the Moon!

To land on the Moon, a spacecraft needs to travel even faster, at a speed of 40,000 k.p.h. as it leaves Earth, and further, about 4,000,000 kms.

A Russian dog called Laika was the first living creature to travel in space in 1957.

Landing on a star which has no atmosphere has to be done very gently, using rocket engines, not parachutes. Then the whole procedure has to be carried out in reverse to take off again...

John F. Kennedy, the President of the United States, threw down an incredible challenge to technology on 25th May 1961: 'America will land a man on the Moon before 1970'.

The challenge was taken up: on 21st July 1969, Neil Armstrong and Edwin Aldrin walked on the surface of the Moon. It was the climax of one of the greatest enterprises of all time: the Apollo space project. In order to achieve it, America built a giant rocket, Saturn V, and a spacecraft capable of landing on the Moon, the Apollo lunar module. In all, twelve Americans were to go to the Moon between 1969 and 1972.

The Apollo command module splashed down in the Pacific Ocean on its return to Earth.

The astronauts used a lunar roving vehicle to travel about on the Moon's surface.

The Apollo lunar module

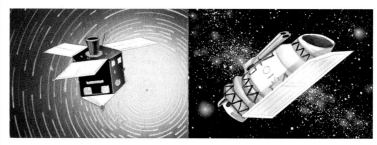

Communication satellites handle all kinds of electronic communications in the form of microwaves. These are telephone calls, radio and television broadcasts, telex and fax messages.

The first satellite, Sputnik, was sent into space on 4th October 1957, powered by the Soviet rocket Zemiorka. The space age had begun.

The first American satellite, Explorer, was launched on 31st January 1958. **Exploring the Moon and travelling through space provides us with important new knowledge.** High above the Earth, in the airless world of space, hundreds of artificial moons, or satellites, circle silently in orbit*, exploring an environment that was quite unknown up till now.

From their orbits, satellites are able to pick up clear signals from the stars before they are distorted by Earth's atmosphere: gamma rays, X and Ultraviolet rays, visible and infrared light, radio waves...

Modern telephones link up through space! Communication satellites, comsats, make it possible for information to travel from one end of the world to the other on super-high-frequency radio waves called microwaves. This is how we can communicate instantly over vast distances.

Man-made satellites don't need engines. Although it is moving through space at 28,000 k.p.h. or more, a satellite has no engine. Just as the Earth moves round the Sun, or the Moon round the Earth, satellites circle our planet continuously. They are in orbit.

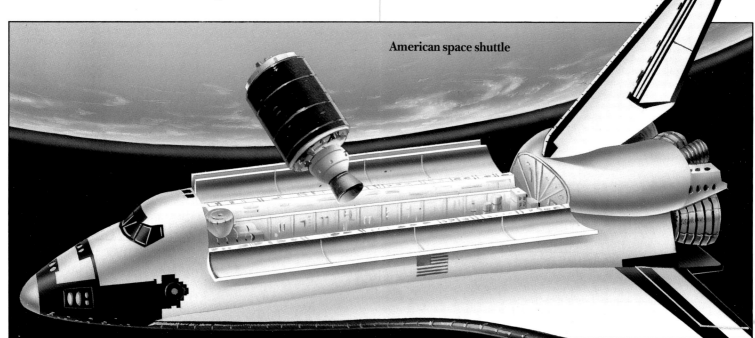

American space shuttle

Observatories in space have revolutionised astronomy.

Now it is possible to watch the birth and death of a star, to probe the heart of the galaxies, to look at quasars, the objects furthest away from us in space. The most important astronomical satellite, the Hubble space telescope, was sent into orbit in 1990. It should be able to pick up objects which are a hundred times less luminous than those we can see through telescopes on Earth.

Earth seen from the Cosmos*

Geostationary satellites move at a certain speed so that they remain always over the same point on the Earth's surface. They look at the formation and break-up of clouds, for instance. 'Satellite pictures' on television weather forecasts are taken by this type of satellite.

Earth survey satellites are not so far away.

They are in orbit at about 700-1,000 kilometres above the Earth and are studying fields, forests, coasts, houses... Spot, a well-known French satellite, takes less than one month to pass over every part of the Earth. The pictures it sends back are detailed enough to show the dimensions of a lorry!

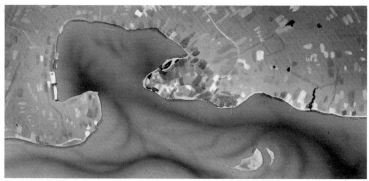

We can look at coastlines and detect pollution from pictures sent to Earth from a satellite.

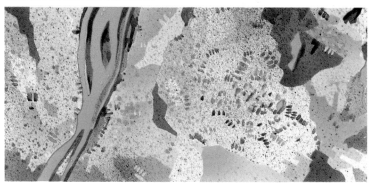

Satellite photographs can be false-coloured to give scientists a geological map of an area.

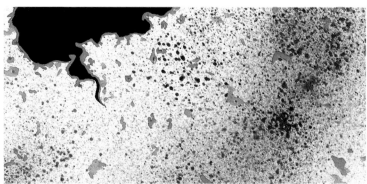

Thanks to earth survey satellites, it is possible to predict harvests, monitor the health of forests and get all sorts of ecological and agricultural information.

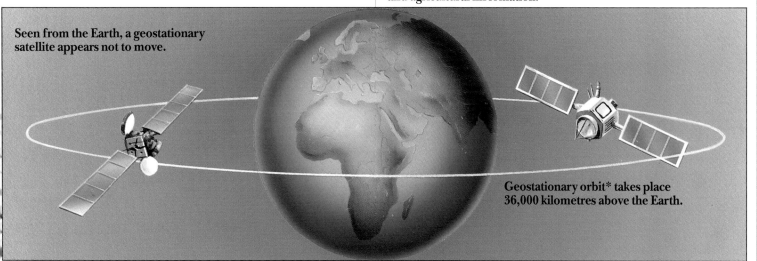

Seen from the Earth, a geostationary satellite appears not to move.

Geostationary orbit* takes place 36,000 kilometres above the Earth.

Will it be possible to build a city in space?

Ariane and Hermes: the Europeans in space

The United States of America and the former Soviet Union took the world into the space age. In a few years' time, men and women will leave Earth in a small space aeroplane called Hermes, developed in Europe, launched by a European rocket, Ariane V. They will be working on an all-European space station, Columbus. The first manned flight is planned for about the year 2000.

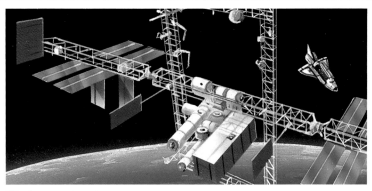

The international space station Freedom will be rather like space Lego, put together from hundreds of small pieces.

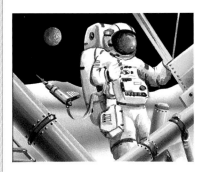

Space stations are growing larger all the time!

The first ones, launched in the 1970s, were about the size of a railway carriage.

The Russian station Mir, which means peace, now looks more like an entire train! It has four 'carriages', known as modules, and soon it will have six. Between two and six men live there for periods ranging from six months to a whole year.

Living in space...

The Americans are planning the space station Freedom. This international project will be made up of two American modules, one European, Columbus, and one Japanese. In the 21st century, these stations may develop to become colonies in space, where hundreds or even thousands of men and women could live.

It may not be long before we land a person on Mars!

Return to the Moon...

Astronauts will probably go back to the Moon at the beginning of the next century. This time, it won't be just a flying visit: mankind will be there to stay. A permanent base would be set up and the Moon would become a scientific observatory. Materials from the Moon could be used for developing industry in space. Solar energy, of which there is a limitless supply in space and on the Moon, would be widely used by the new space factories and also by people on Earth.

Objective: Mars!

The biggest aim of mankind's adventures in space is the famous red planet, Mars. Is there, or has there ever been, life on Mars? We already know that the climate there has been very dry and cold. But Mars has not always been a frozen desert. Rivers once flowed, and it still has mounds of ice. Perhaps there is water deep underground! If any trace of life were to be found, it would be of great significance. It will probably be in your lifetime, around the year 2020, that astronauts first set foot on the red planet. The third millenium heralds a new challenge for mankind: the Cosmos* will be opened up to discovery, and who knows what inventions lie in store!

The first astronauts to arrive on Mars might stay there several months. Although they will reach the red planet in a large spaceship, they will probably land on it in a small capsule.

It is the year 2010. Astronauts in space-suits are building the first city on the Moon.

Games and activities, a quiz, intriguing facts, sayings, a glossary, followed by the index

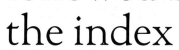

Travelling and measuring

Man's wish to travel faster and further

led to the invention of the rudder, the wheel, the steam engine, electricity. Using these, people were able to explore the world and conquer new lands.

A wheel dating from 2,000 BC

This map shows the world as Europeans knew it around the year AD 1600.

They had yet to explore Greenland and northern Asia, and had not travelled into the heart of America. From the end of the 15th century, Spanish ships regularly crossed the Atlantic, and the Portuguese rounded the southern tip of Africa on their route to India and the exotic Spice Islands. Gradually, they established colonies in these new countries, first on the coasts and then further and further inland. From these distant lands merchants brought back goods that could not be produced in Europe: silk, spices, perfumes, cotton, sugar cane, cocoa beans and thousands of other things as well.

At the same time, the British and the Dutch began to open up trade routes overseas.

In 1600, Queen Elizabeth I chartered the famous East India Company, which was given exclusive trading rights between England and the Far East.

In 1620, the Mayflower set sail from Plymouth for Massachusetts, to found the first colony in North America.

Map of the world around 1600

Christopher Columbus

Vasco da Gama

Ferdinand Mage

Jacques Cartier

What is speed?

It is the relationship between a distance and the time taken to cover that distance. Speed is most usually calculated in kilometres per hour.

In the past, sailors used to work out the speed of a ship by using a rope with knots tied in it at regular intervals. We say a boat is travelling at 10 knots when it has travelled 10 nautical miles in one hour.
1 nautical mile = 1,852 m.

When there is a storm raging, how hard is the wind blowing?

Wind speed is measured by using an anemometer. There is also the Beaufort scale (from 0-12), worked out by Admiral Beaufort. A fresh breeze would be Force 4, but bad weather's coming if it rises to Force 8 or 9. Some cars can travel at speeds of 300 k.p.h., but the aircraft Concorde can travel faster than the speed of sound, Mach speed, that's about 1,220 k.p.h.

Sunshine and rain

Measuring cold and heat, dryness and humidity, forecasting variations in our climate, are all part of the science of meteorology, which makes use of very sophisticated instruments like geostationary satellites. Forecasting the weather may be interesting for any of us, but for sailors, aircraft pilots and farmers the information may be of vital importance.

Thermometers

The centigrade system, invented by Celsius, takes the freezing point of water as 0°C, and the boiling point as 100°C. In the system thought up by the physicist Fahrenheit, water freezes at 32°F and boils at 212°F. Thermometers show the temperature by means of mercury or alcohol, which expand or contract inside a glass tube as it gets hotter or colder.

Barometers show changes in air pressure.

The weather is very much affected by air pressure which is measured in millibars. The needle on the barometer moves as the pressure changes. The mercury barometer, was invented by the Italian physicist, Evangelista Torricelli, in 1643.

Canals are man-made waterways.

Some form a link between two seas or two regions, some help with irrigation, bringing water to areas where it is in short supply. The level of a canal must remain even all along its length. This may mean digging through hills and building aqueducts across valleys. If the land is too uneven, locks have to be built between levels.

Why do trains travel on the left?

Long before railways were invented, English knights who met on horseback in a narrow lane would each keep to the left, so their swords would not clash. Since the first railway engineers were British, the practice was adopted in most parts of the world, even though in most countries road users drive on the right.

The canal at Corinth, in Greece, links the Aegean Sea with the Ionian Sea. This enormous cutting took 10 years to complete.

A boat drives into a lock, and the gates close behind it.

The sluice gates open and water flows into the lock chamber.

When the water level has risen to the same level as outside the lock, the gates open and the boat moves through.

The system can be operated in reverse when the boat is travelling in the opposite direction.

The wheels of the future will turn in space!

They won't be rolling along roads, but will be guiding spacecraft and satellites as they orbit the Earth, observing it and taking photographs...

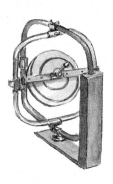

Electromagnets make the wheel in a satellite turn very fast, because they cut down on friction and wear and tear. This also means there is less risk of a breakdown. As the wheel speeds up or slows down, the satellite changes direction.

Space aeroplane Hermes transported by an Airbus

Hermes in flight

Rocket Ariane

Daily life, daily pleasures

Clothes are a human invention too!
Prehistoric tribespeople used needles made of bone to sew skins together with animal sinews. The first metal needles appeared around 3,000 BC.

By that time, the Chinese already knew how to weave silk thread produced by caterpillars, and the Egyptians gathered hemp to make into tunics. We don't know who invented spinning and weaving. Both take a long time, and need skill and patience.

For many hundreds of years, it was the women's task to make the clothes that their families wore. Only the rich could afford to go to tailors and dressmakers.
The first sewing machines appeared in 1830. They were used to make military uniforms.

Music has not always been written down in the same way. From top to bottom: musical score from the 15th century, score from the 20th century and modern music

Where did music and musical instruments come from?
Music, song and dance seem to have been part of ceremony and celebration since the earliest times. The first musical instruments were made out of objects that were in everyday use: an earthenware pot covered with an animal skin made a drum, a reed pierced with holes became a flute.
Up until the Middle Ages, people learned songs by hearing them repeated: there was no way of writing down the notes. But then music began to grow more and more complicated, and if people were going to be able to remember it, they had to find a way of writing it down. A Benedictine monk had the idea of inscribing signs on a stave of four lines, to show the pitch of each note and how long it should be held. Gradually, the system was improved, and musicians were able to compose pieces for many instruments.

The first public concerts were held in the 17th century. Before then, orchestras only ever played in the royal courts of kings and princes.

Who taught you to play?
No-one! All babies play with anything they can get hold of. Play is a way of learning about the world around you and gaining skills. As you grow up, you play with more complicated toys.

Many of the games we play have their roots way back in the past. In the Middle Ages, children played hide-and-seek and blind man's buff, as well as charades and dances with actions, like nursery rhymes. People also played chess and draughts, and card games.

Made from cloth, wood or china, dolls have existed for as long as there have been children, but the first teddy bears were made in 1900.

■ Quiz

Can you answer these questions? The answers are at the bottom of the page.

1. In which country was the compass invented?
a) China
b) India
c) Portugal

2. When did windmills first appear in Europe?
a) in Roman times
b) in the Middle Ages
c) in the 19th century

3. The first writing we know of was done by...
a) the Egyptians
b) the Sumerians
c) the Americans

4. Christopher Columbus crossed the Atlantic in 1492 in a ship called...
a) Santa Maria
b) Santa Barbara
c) Hermione the Great

5. The first living creature to be sent into space was...
a) a monkey
b) a rabbit
c) a dog

6. The first railway line was built in...
a) France
b) Scotland
c) England

7. The first man to walk on the Moon was called...
a) Yuri Gagarin
b) Neil Armstrong
c) John Kennedy

Answers:
1.a 2.b 3.b 4.a 5.c 6.c 7.b

Would you like to play a game with these fierce pirates?
Help them open the door of their cave. First, you need to discover the password. You can make it up from the letters printed in heavy type on the rocks. Then find the key that fits the keyhole.

What is hidden behind these rocks? A fabulous animal?

A poor prisoner?

Coffers full of gold doubloons?

Sapphires and rubies?

Rivers of diamonds?

The password is 'treasure'. The right key is no. 4.

1   2   3   4   5   6   7   8

■ True or false?

1. Champollion was a great archaeologist who discovered temples in Ancient Greece.

2. The first text that Gutenberg printed, in about 1450, was a newspaper.

3. The inventor of the phonograph, an early type of record player, was deaf.

4. Aspirin is made out of extracts from the willow tree.

5. The reflective studs used to mark traffic lanes on roads were invented by William Catsize.

6. Coca-cola was first sold in chemists' shops as a brain tonic.

7. Laser beams were invented by Mr Laser.

Expressions connected with measuring keep cropping up. Do you know these ones?

'For good measure' means something extra added to what is due.
If something's 'made to measure', it fits well and suits a person perfectly.
'Give him an inch, and he'll take a mile' means he will take advantage of you, given the chance.
Milestones were set along a road to mark off each mile; now the expression means a significant event or stage in your life.

■ Games

Make your own cartoon: Happy Man, Sad Man.
Take a long, thin piece of paper and fold it in the middle.

Draw a laughing face on the top half and a sad face underneath, towards the end furthest from the fold.

Roll the top part round a pencil, then move the pencil to left and right very quickly; your little man won't know whether to laugh or cry!

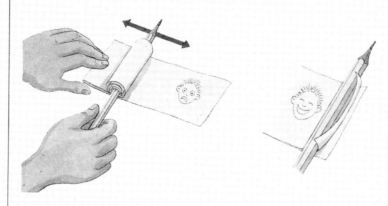

A flicker-book
Take a pad of paper and draw an animal in the bottom right-hand corner of the last page, then draw it moving very slightly on each page till you get to the top.

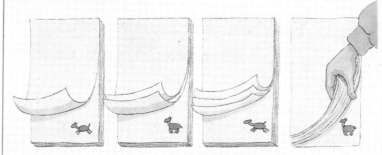

As you flick the pages, your animal will skip and run!

Topsy-turvy
You need a small cardboard disc, two pieces of string, and a pen.
On one side of the disc, draw a dog with his mouth open; on the other side of the disc, draw him with his mouth shut.

Make a hole on each side of the disc and thread a piece of string through. Twist the string as tightly as you can, then let it unwind as you hold the string taut between your fingers. The disc will spin round. What happens to the dog?

Answers to True or False

1. False. Champollion was the first to work out how to read hieroglyphics, the writing of the Ancient Egyptians.
2. False. The first text he printed was the Bible.
3. True. He was called Edison and he became deaf at 14.
4. True. It was the German chemist, Adolph von Bayer, who first made the extracts into tablets, in 1893, although willow had been recognised as medicinal since the time of Ancient Greece.
5. False. They were invented by Percy Shaw in 1934. They reflect the light of car head-lamps just as a cat's eyes do.
6. True. Coca-cola was concocted in 1886 by American pharmacist Dr John Pemberton. The recipe still contains a mystery ingredient.
7. False. LASER is made from the initials Light Amplification by Stimulated Emission of Radiation.

■ Did you know?

Gunpowder
Just like paper and the compass, gunpowder was a Chinese invention. The Chinese used it to make flaming arrows in wartime, and fireworks. The secret formula was stolen from the Chinese by the Mongols and then passed to the Arabs, who used it against the Europeans during the Crusades. The first cannons were used in Europe in the 15th century.

Fireworks

The Scandinavians taught us to ski!
People in cold mountain regions had always used skis to get about on snow. In 1888 the Norwegian Nansen crossed Greenland on skis. The sport was developed as techniques of turning and racing were perfected. The first international competition was held in 1921.

The first proper anaesthetic was used to put patients to sleep for operations in 1846, in Boston, USA, by Dr William Morton. Charles Jackson had discovered that ether was an anaesthetic in 1841.

The X ray was discovered in 1895, by the German physicist Wilhelm Roentgen. Soon doctors began using X rays to see inside the human body. In 1903, the German surgeon, George Perthes, discovered that X rays slow down or stop the growth of cancer. Today X ray treatment is used widely against cancers; we call it radiotherapy.

Louis Pasteur, the French chemist who gave his name to pasteurisation, developed vaccines from 1879. He discovered that if weakened bacteria were injected into the body they stimulated the body's own defences to protect it from illness. Thanks to vaccines, we can now immunise people against many of the most dangerous diseases like smallpox, tuberculosis, tetanus, diphtheria, polio, anthrax and rabies.

Penicillin was named by Alexander Fleming in 1928. He noticed that a mould had killed some of the bacteria on a dish in his laboratory. He found that the mould produced a substance which killed certain bacteria in humans without damaging white blood cells. It was an important milestone in the treatment of disease and infection: antibiotics had been discovered.

The refrigerator was the most brilliant idea!
If food is chilled it can be stored much longer and still be good to eat. Long ago, people realised that ice is useful: in medieval times, people collected ice in winter and buried it in deep holes. Later, ships were sent to bring pieces off icebergs to European ports. In about 1850, scientists found that low temperatures could be created through chemical procedures. Charles Tellier, a Frenchman, invented a refrigerator which used ammonia; as it dissolved in water, the ammonia absorbed heat and produced cold.

Who invented matches?
Until the middle of the 19th century, people lit candles with slender tapers soaked in sulphur, which had to be touched to another flame. In 1830 in France, Charles Suria added white phosphorus to the tip of a small stick of wood, which ignited when struck against a surface coated with sulphur and potassium chlorate. But white phosphorus is poisonous; later it was replaced by red phosphorus. Modern matches had been invented.

■ Inventors of genius

Many inventors of crucial inventions, landmarks of progress, remain anonymous or are lost in legend. But the names of more recent inventors are well-known.

Gutenberg (1398-1467)
He was German, and a goldsmith by trade. The Chinese had invented printing, but Gutenberg discovered the most practical way to use it. In Europe, people were already printing wood engravings, which were made into books. Now Gutenberg invented movable metal type, which he fixed on a frame. Letters could be moved about and re-used.

William Caxton (1422-1491)
In 1476, he set up the first printing press in England. Caxton printed a great number of books. Most of them were in English, not Latin, which up till then had been the standard printed language. Caxton translated many of them himself. One of the first large books to be printed was Chaucer's *Canterbury Tales*.

Alessandro Volta (1745-1827)
The electric battery was his invention. His voltaic cell of 1800 was made up of discs of copper and zinc linked to a bath of salt water. It did produce electricity, but it was very unwieldy!

Jacques Daguerre (1787-1851)
He has been nicknamed the father of the photograph. In 1835, together with another scientist, Nicephore Niepce, he discovered a way of developing and fixing an image taken by a camera. The films he used were copper plates coated with silver iodide; these turned black when exposed to light, and recorded an image. To develop the image, Daguerre dipped the plate in a chemical known as the 'developer', then fixed it with a solution of common salt. The image then became permanent.

Samuel Morse (1791-1872)
An American painter, who later became an inventor. He perfected a system of transmitting messages by means of electric signals. His alphabet, known as the Morse Code, was made up simply of short dots and long dashes. It could be read, heard, or seen from a distance, and shipping has made very good use of it. The letters SOS (3 short, 3 long, 3 short) form the international distress signal.

Thomas Edison (1847-1931)
An American, born into a poor family, he started his career by selling newspapers, but by the time he died, he had many inventions to his name. At the age of 14, he became deaf, but this disability did not stop him from inventing the phonograph in 1877. It was a device which could reproduce sounds. A cylinder turned, and a needle reproduced the vibrations made by a human voice. Edison also founded the first cinema studio.

Alexander Bell (1847-1922)
Born in Scotland, he started by teaching sign language to deaf and dumb children. As he tried different ways of helping the deaf hear, he concentrated on the vibrations made by the human voice. He succeeded in transmitting a sound down an electric wire, and this finally led to the invention of the telephone in 1876.

Rudolph Diesel (1858-1913)
He began his career as a refrigeration engineer. He noticed that the steam engines of his day were not very powerful and, in 1893, he attempted the first experiments with an engine that worked on fuel oil, igniting by compression of air and not from an electric spark. He has given his name to all engines that work on diesel oil.

Diesel engines are more efficient than petrol engines, but tend to be quite heavy. They are mainly used in large vehicles.

■ Glossary

Amber: fossilised resin. Its Greek name, *elektron*, gives us *electricity*.

Aluminium: a soft, white, very lightweight metal, often used in building aircraft bodies.

Cam: a piece of wood or metal, shaped to fit into a wheel, so that circular motion is transformed into up-and-down motion, or vice versa.

Caravel: small, sturdy boat with three sails, riding high in the water, and carrying a crew of about 20 men.

Circuit (electric): wire pathway, usually copper, from a power source and back again. The power source might be an electromagnetic generator or a battery.

Cosmos: the universe seen as an ordered whole, from the Greek word *kosmos*, meaning world.

Crank: rod bent at right-angles for converting a circular movement to an up-and-down motion.

to Domesticate: to tame wild animals and bring them under human control. Pets and farm animals are domesticated.

Economy: the organised system by which a society orders its banking, industry, trade and commerce.

Environmentalist: someone whose study and work involve caring for our planet and safeguarding the future of all living things.

to Forge: to shape metal by heating it in the fire and hammering it as it cools.

Fossil: plant or animal remains which have been preserved in the earth for many thousands of years until they turned to stone, but which can be recognised for what they were.

Gauge: the distance between the rails of a railway line. The standard gauge for most European countries is 1.4 metres. Problems were encountered by early railway engineers before the gauge was standardised. What were they to do when rails of two different companies met? Passengers and freight had to be loaded and then re-loaded, a tiresome business.

Hawker: a travelling salesman. Centuries ago, when shops were still rare, hawkers went from village to village carrying needles and thread, lace, pots, books.

Interest: the sum of money paid by the borrower to the lender in return for the loan.

Latitude: position on the Earth north or south of the Equator.

Longitude: position on the Earth east or west of the Greenwich Meridian.

to Mine: to dig into the ground to extract metal or

coal. Open-cast mines exploit metal or coal reserves near the surface. Deeper reserves need to be mined via a vertical shaft.

Nugget: small rough lump of natural gold or other precious metal.

Orbit: repeated, curved course of a planet or satellite around another object in space. To orbit something means to go around it in orbit. Our planet orbits the Sun.

Phoenicians: a great trading nation covering part of what is now Lebanon and Syria in the Middle East, at the height of their power from the 14th to the 9th centuries BC. Through trade, they linked the old civilisations of Egypt and Mesopotamia with the newer powers of the Mediterranean. They even came to Cornwall.

Photoelectric cells: Devices that use electrons emitted by light-sensitive metals to generate an electrical current.

Photovoltaic cells: contain crystals of silicon. They are recharged by light. They were first made for spacecraft, but now they often power watches or calculators.

Porcelain: fine, delicate china made from white clay called kaolin mixed with powdered granite.

Spices: extracts of aromatic plants used to flavour food, such as ginger, cumin, cinnamon, cloves... often grown in distant, hot countries.

Starboard: the right hand side of a ship. Before the invention of the stern rudder, ships were steered by a rudder on the right, or 'steerboard' side. This became 'starboard'. Because of the projecting rudder, it was

impossible for a ship to tie up at port on that side, so the other side, the left, became known as the port side.

Stock Exchange: a huge market, where stocks and shares in businesses round the world are bought and sold. The London Stock Exchange is the oldest in the world.

Sub-soil: soil lying just below the surface soil, and often of poor quality.

Tidal power station: When the motion of the tides is channelled by an estuary, it produces a very strong flow of water. Tidal power is harnessed by building a dam across the tidal flow. Some environmentalists object to this form of power, saying it damages the wetlands and the wildfowl that depend on them.

to Typeset: to arrange letters and spaces ready for printing on a press. Movable type was put in place, one letter at a time, by skilled compositors, but nowadays much typesetting is done on computers.

Valve: a sort of plug that opens and closes automatically.

Watt: electrical unit of power named after the Scottish engineer, James Watt (1736-1819).

Wavelength: distance from the crest of one wave to the crest of the next.

Here is a list of museums and historical sites you could visit. Your local library will give you more information.

Museum of Technology
Riverside
Cambridge

Narrow Gauge Railway Museum
Wharf Station
Neptune Road
Tywyn
Gwynedd

National Museum of Photography,
  Film and TV
Prince's View
Bradford

Science Museum
Exhibition Road
South Kensington
London SW7

Shuttleworth Collection
Old Warden Aerodrome
Nr Biggleswade
Bedfordshire

Bluebell Railway
Sheffield Park Station
Nr Uckfield
East Sussex

Bank of England Museum
Bank of England
Bartholomew Lane
London EC3

Museum of the Moving Image
South Bank
London SE1

Heritage Motor Museum
Syon Park
Brentford

London Transport Museum
Covent Garden
London WC2

St Bride Printing Library
St Bride Institute
Bride Lane
London EC4

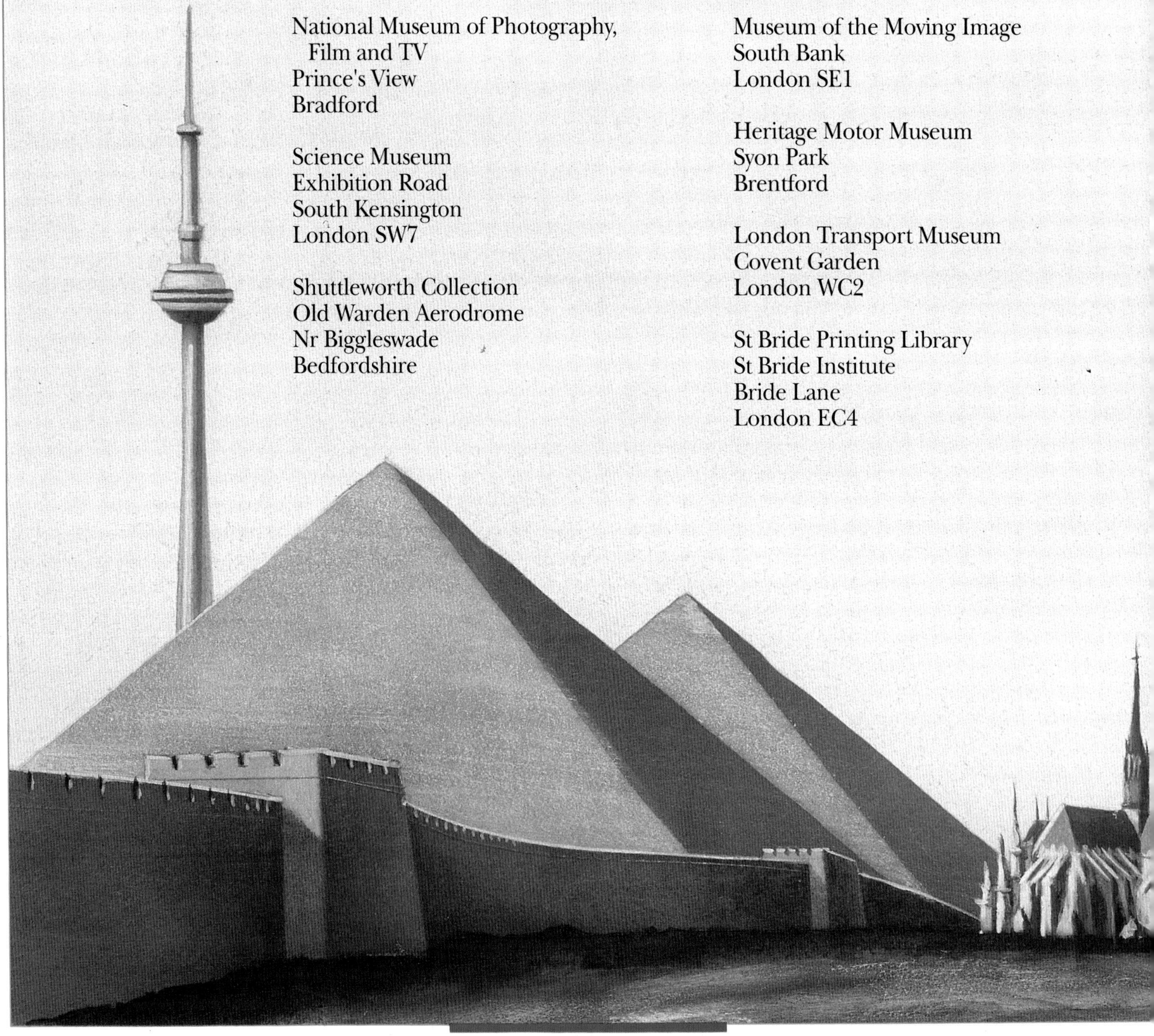

In Australia:

Museum of Applied Arts
and Sciences
Powerhouse
Ultimo
Sydney 2007

National Science and Technology
Centre (Questacon)
Edward Terrace
Parkes
Australian Capital Territory 2600

National Motor Museum
Birdwood
South Australia 5234

National Film and Sound Archives
McCoy Crescent
Acton
Australian Capital Territory 2601

Banking and Currency Museum
3 Graves Street
Kadina
South Australia 5554

In Canada:

Science World of British Columbia
1455 Quebec Street
Vancouver
British Columbia
V6B 5E7

Ontario Science Centre
770 Don Mills Road
Don Mills
Ontario
M3C 1T3

National Museum of Science
and Technology
1867 Boulevard St Laurent
Ottawa
Ontario
K1G 5A3

The entries in **bold** refer to whole chapters on the subject.